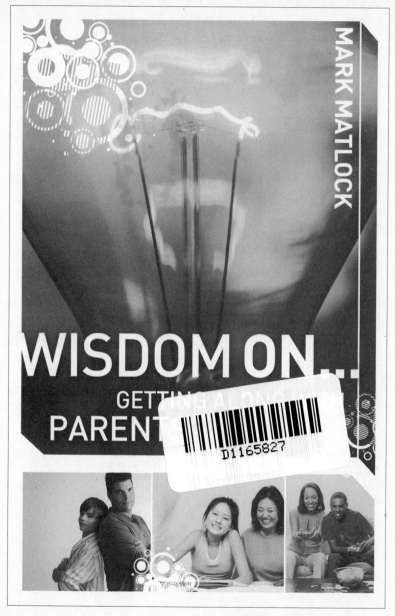

MARK MATLOCK

WISDOM ON...
GETTING ALONG WITH
PARENTS

D1165827

 **ZONDERVAN**®

 ZONDERVAN.com/
AUTHORTRACKER
follow your favorite authors

 in:vert

 youth
specialties

youth specialties

Wisdom On...Getting Along with Parents
Copyright 2008 by Mark Matlock

Youth Specialties resources, 300 S. Pierce St., El Cajon, CA 92020 are published by Zondervan, 5300 Patterson Ave. SE, Grand Rapids, MI 49530.

ISBN 978-0-310-27929-7

Web site addresses listed in this book were current at the time of publication. Please contact Youth Specialties via e-mail (YS@YouthSpecialties.com) to report URLs that are no longer operational and replacement URLs if available.

Cover design by SharpSeven Design
Interior design by David Conn

Printed in the United States of America

08 09 10 11 12 • 16 15 14 13 12 11 10 9 8 7 6 5 4 3 2 1

This book is dedicated to my grandparents, George and Nora Matlock and Ray and Ruth Albrecht. They were good friends before my parents fell in love, and they helped start the church I grew up in. Not only have they been essential in my spiritual growth and maturity, they made MY parents!

TABLE OF CONTENTS

A big thanks to everyone who has helped make this series a reality: Chris Lyon, fellow friend and writer; Randy Southern, for excellent editing and feedback; Holly Sharp, for the cool covers; Roni Meek and Jay Howver at Youth Specialties; and the others I haven't met who had to correct my spelling and punctuation. Thank you all. You make your parents proud.

ACKNOWLEDGMENTS

CHAPTER 1

WISDOM ON PARENTS?
REALLY?

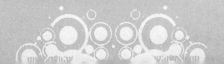

My dad and I had been working outside all Saturday morning. My father loves to prune trees and bushes, and on our three acres there were plenty of trees and bushes to clip.

On this particular Saturday morning, I'd been recruited to help my dad—whether I liked it or not. My job was to deliver wheelbarrow after wheelbarrow full of clippings to the dumpster. The piles seemed endless to me. And my father had no intention of stopping. Needless to say, I was less than thrilled about spending my Saturday doing yard work.

When the dumpster was full, I assumed we were done for the day. So when my dad moved on to another tree, my blood started to boil.

"Let's take a break for a moment," my father finally suggested. As we sat in the shade, my dad started giving me a hard time about my attitude. He knew I wasn't happy, but his feeble attempts to cheer me up only fueled my frustration. Then something bad happened.

My dad started mimicking my pouting face, and I decided I'd had enough. In the heat of the moment, I did something I'd never done before—and have never done since. I *punched* my father—right in the chest.

He was stunned. I was stunned. Hitting was unacceptable in my family. Where had my violent outburst come from? I didn't pause to wonder. Instead, I started running. And my dad started running after me.

My dad hadn't chased me since I was in elementary school, but I remembered that I'd never been able to get away from him. He always caught me. But things had changed since then. Now I was 15 years old, and my dad was also

much older. And I was on the track and field team at my high school.

I sprinted across our three acres to a corner of the property furthest from our house. I didn't look back because I was afraid that if I did, I'd see my dad's arm reaching out to grab me. But when I got to the fence at the back of the property, I had no choice. I was out of options. So I turned around to find that my dad was...not even close to me.

He was about an acre away, hunched over, and huffing and puffing. I had outrun my father.

Despite the seriousness of the situation, I couldn't help smiling. I'd beaten my dad! All my life, he'd won every competition we'd ever had. Board games, tennis, basketball—he beat me at everything. Finally, though, the tables had turned. I'd beaten him at something.

My dad stood up, smiled at me, and waved as I did a little victory dance. And that made me reconsider my situation. Why had my dad smiled at me? Why did he walk back to the house?

I sat down on a clump of grass and reviewed my circumstances. I had won; he had lost. But I was sitting alone in the field, and he was in the house! I knew at some point I was going to have to face him. I couldn't stay in the field all day...or could I?

My dad had smiled because he knew I'd have to return home eventually. And then I'd have to deal with the consequences of my actions. I learned the hard way that in a battle between parent and kid, there's rarely a clear-cut winner. I hope I can offer you some chunks of wisdom to help you in your relationship with your parents.

As I travel around the country and speak to students in person—as well as online—I hear a lot of talk about parents. And the things I hear aren't all that different from the things my friends and I said about our parents.

"I love my parents, but..."

"They just don't understand me."

"They think I'm still a kid."

"They don't get what it's like to be a kid these days."

"I can't stand how they try to control everything I do."

"Why don't they listen to what I say?"

"Why can't they understand that I just want to be left alone?"

"Why do they have to make such a big deal out of everything?"

"What if they're wrong?"

At some point most students will have to deal with tough times in their relationships with their parents. And when a serious conflict occurs, it can have a huge impact on your life. It can affect every other relationship you have. It can cause you to doubt yourself. It can make you question everything you thought you could take for granted. Like it or not, the way you deal with your parents will become a cornerstone of the rest of your life.

For all of its importance, though, I've found that students aren't very interested in hearing about how to get along with their parents. They'd much rather hear God's wisdom regarding sex and dating, or movies and music, or making money.

Why is there so little interest in an issue as important or vital as your first—and probably longest-lasting—relationship? For one thing, most students believe they're doing just fine with their moms and dads, thankyouverymuch. Recent surveys reveal that teenagers and parents are pretty happy together, for the most part. Despite the fact that most students will go through a rough time with the 'rents, the majority say they're in an okay place at any given moment. So why talk about fixing what seemingly isn't broken? For starters, being "okay" isn't always the same thing as living wisely in relation to our parents—but we'll cover more on that later.

On the other side of the coin, many students who are currently on the outs with Mom and Dad don't want to hear me talk about God's wisdom on the issue because they're convinced they already know what I'm going to say: "Your parents are right. You're wrong. So be quiet and do what they say." Actually, that's not what I say—but there will be more on that subject a little later as well.

Please understand me: This book is NOT about getting you to fall in line and be a good little soldier in your parents' army. It's NOT about trying to fix your behavior issues at home. It's NOT about convincing you that your parents are right about everything. It's NOT about making you believe it's all *your* problem if you have an issue with your folks.

Like all the other books in the *Wisdom On...* series, this one is about finding a life that matters by learning to live wisely. If you've read any of those other books (on sex and dating, media, money, and other topics), then you know I'm passionate about God's wisdom. You know wisdom doesn't just mean, "Do whatever the Bible says, and you'll be okay." That's true to a point, but wisdom involves much more than mindless rule-following.

We live in a time when people have more access to information than at any other point in the planet's history. The

Internet has changed everything. You can know whatever there is to know about any given topic at any hour of any day. Your generation has become experts at managing the constant barrage of information—facts, figures, stats, data, and more data. And it's not all just cold, hard intelligence. You're also constantly processing emotional and relationship information. With Web sites such as Facebook and MySpace, you can quantify and organize all of your "friends" on a Web page. Your world is digitized, sorted, and searchable. (By the way, if you're on MySpace or Facebook, look me up. I'll add you as my friend.)

Wisdom isn't information. It isn't raw knowledge. Wisdom is the ability to take all of the data—all of the input—and make some sense of it. Wisdom is the ability to hold on to information and use it to make good choices—choices that matter. Put enough wise choices together, and you'll find yourself standing knee-deep in a life worth living—instead of just floating along on an ocean of confusing ideas and possibilities. More than ever, people need wisdom—and we need it right now.

You might have guessed by now that we're not talking about Zen wisdom. We're not talking about the wisdom of nature. We're not talking about Wall Street wisdom. I'm convinced that the only worthwhile source of wisdom is God. Why? Because God designed the universe and everything in it. To really understand what's going on in the world, you have to start with the user manual. And the only one qualified to write that Manual (the Bible) is the One who made everything in the first place.

Learning God's wisdom is the key to understanding...everything. That includes your parents. You need God's wisdom to figure out how your relationship with Mom and Dad is supposed to work now that you're no longer a kid, but you're not quite an adult either. You need God's wisdom to figure out how to honor and obey Mom and Dad while you're also breaking away from them.

You'll be surprised by some of the things I call *wisdom*. Some readers will discover they need to listen to their parents LESS. Some will discover extremely effective strategies for getting their folks to give them MORE freedom. And a few will realize they can use their parents' most glaring weaknesses to make life better in the long run.

Becoming wise about your relationship with Mom and Dad will be a lot easier if you can find some empathy (or the ability to feel what they feel) for them. Let's start with that in the next chapter.

CHAPTER 2
IMAGINE THAT!

I'm going to ask you to do something that might seem a little childish, but it's actually really helpful. If we were in the same room together, then I'd dim the lights, maybe cue up some chill atmospheric music, and ask you to close your eyes. That might make it tough to keep reading this book, though, so you'll have to do this imaginative exercise with your eyes open.

Think about where you are in your life right now—today. Is it summer? Are you in school? Start there. Now start scrolling through your future (as you imagine it) a few months at a time. One school year ends, another begins. How are your grades? Are you participating in any sports? Music? Drama? Are you working many hours? Do you like school? Hate it?

Now imagine your senior year starts, and you find yourself extremely attracted to someone of the opposite sex. You fall hard for this person right away. It takes the person a little while to warm up to you; but when it finally happens, you're crazy about each other. You can't imagine being any happier. Are you imagining this? Maybe you're thinking of someone you know right now. Maybe you see a person you haven't yet met. What color is the person's hair? What does the person look like? Is the person funny? Athletic? Smart?

Months roll by. Now you're in college. The two of you are growing closer all the time. You spend a lot of hours together. The rest of your life involves plenty of studying, working, hanging out with friends, maybe going to church. You wrestle with figuring out what you should do with your life. More school? A career? Something else? You're older and maybe a little wiser, but you still struggle with some of the same issues that got you down back in middle school. On the up side, you're having a blast living on your own, making your own choices, staying up 'til all hours, and packing your life with everything you can think of that's fun, meaningful, and worth doing.

Still, it always comes back to this person you're in love with. Sometimes you fight, but that's because you both care so much about the relationship. Eventually, you both realize you want to spend the rest of your lives together. After some romance and way too much drama, you find yourselves standing in a church, looking into each other's eyes, and saying "I do."

Like all newly married couples, you quickly discover two undeniable facts: Life is great together, and life is really hard together. You fight about stupid things sometimes, and you realize in a new way just how selfish you are—and how selfish your spouse is. You *want* to make right choices, but you don't always do it. You still have to work, maybe study, clean the bathroom, and figure out what to eat and how much to spend. You have some amazing times you'll never forget, but you also have some big issues in life and in your relationship that you just can't seem to get past.

Now I want you to think about the place where you live. It's not your dream house. (You're still too young for that.) It might be an apartment. It might be a little place that's not located in the best part of town.

Now think about some of your friends. (I'm talking about your current friends.) Think how they'll be several years from now. They're also grown up and living on their own. Some are married. A couple of them might be divorced already. Some are starting to have kids.

Some of your friends continue to make really lousy decisions. You still like them a lot, but they have a tendency to let people down. They don't seem much wiser than they did all those years ago (way back when you were the age you are right now). Other friends are doing better. Which friends do you imagine living wisely in the future? Which ones aren't living so wisely? Why? (Side note: You might be really surprised by who ends up where 10 years from now.)

Back to you. You really want to be happy, to get along with your spouse, and to make good choices about money and time and work. And you do—for the most part—but it's difficult. Then one day you learn that the two of you are going to have a baby. It's exciting. You spend a lot of time picking out names and figuring out how to make your lives work with the addition of a newborn.

On the day the child is born, something happens that you never expected. You have this incredibly powerful emotional response to the baby. You immediately feel an attachment that's like some kind of overwhelming emotional superglue. You instantly know you'd do anything to keep this child safe. You'd die for this baby without a second thought. I'm talking about an unbreakable spiritual, biological, and emotional bond. You've heard people talk about it before, but you never saw it coming. (You'll just have to take my word for it.)

Suddenly you realize you're laughing more. You feel joyful more often. Having this child in your family really makes you happy. But that intense love isn't enough to make life easy. You have to change everything now. Either you or your spouse will have to stop working, work less, or find someone to watch the baby while you're both working.

You're always worried about the baby getting hurt or not eating right or not sleeping well. You have less time to spend with your spouse. There's a lot less romance and sex going on in your relationship because you're both so busy and tired. Sometimes your love for the baby gets mixed up with anger over how your whole life now revolves around your child almost completely. You're unbelievably proud of this kid—but you're also more stressed out than you've ever been.

As the baby grows, you continue to worry. *Am I working too much? Can we make enough money to support our family? Is our child attending a good enough school? Watching too much TV? Getting enough exercise?* When other kids come along, the process starts all over again. Sometimes you don't even care about the decisions you have to make concerning bedtimes and baths and clothes and food. But someone has to make them. So you use your best judgment and just hope it's okay.

You get mad when your child won't listen to you, mostly because you know you're working really hard to do the best you can for him or her. But you also know all kids are like that. You don't want to be a dictator, but you want your child to learn to make good choices. You feel as though you're always trying to figure out the balance between being too strict and being too easy to push around.

Now your kids are teenagers, and conflict becomes a way of life. You can remember some things about being their age (the age you are right now). And you can remember what your parents were like at that time. You want to do better than your parents did, but you're afraid you're doing worse. You still have the superglue instinct to protect your kids, but you know you have to let them go a little bit more every day.

You start to realize how much your parents are like you. In many ways, they're grown-up teenagers who are doing their best, but they also realize they're a long way from perfect. They have no special training, no expertise in parenting. They're just regular people who hope they've done okay—and hope even harder that their kids learn to live wisely in a really difficult world.

The point of this imagination exercise is NOT to make you feel sorry for your parents or to convince you to put them on a pedestal. I know that some students who are reading this book have parents who've been abusive or who've walked away from their families. Some parents respond to the pressures of family life in very destructive ways. And even those who turn out to be great parents sometimes make some hurtful choices along the way.

Still, our little visual exercise represents the experience of many parents. As kids we don't often think of our folks as regular people who are struggling. But it's really helpful to realize that your parents—whoever they are and whatever they're like right now—started on the road to parenthood from the same place in life that you're at today. It's likely they weren't any smarter or dumber than you are right now. And it's also likely they didn't receive any more special training in how to be a parent than you'll get between now and the time when you have your first child.

Building a wise relationship with your parents starts with seeing them not as *just* the people who run your life and take care of you. It starts with realizing they're people just like you.

Next, you have to understand what God has asked your folks to do as parents. It's a harder job than you might think.

CHAPTER 3

WHAT GOD TELLS YOUR PARENTS TO DO

Most kids have a limited perspective when it comes to their parents, and it's hard for them to be objective. After all, for the first few years of life, a child's relationship with his or her parents is completely one-sided. Mom and Dad do literally everything for their children: change their diapers, help them go to sleep, put food in their mouths, and constantly monitor them for signs of illness.

As kids get a little older, it's natural for them to idolize their parents. The parents are the ones who provide for every single need in the kids' lives. And when the kids are old enough to start wanting things that may not be good for them, the parents decide what's allowed and what's not. In the early years Mom and Dad are the ultimate authorities for everything in the universe.

Such complete dependence raises an interesting question: Who in the world is qualified to make so many vital decisions in another person's life? The truth is, no one is perfectly qualified because no one is perfect. That's why it's safe to say that at some time every parent fails his or her child on some level. It's just a fact of life. Parents are people, and people are *not* perfect.

I have several friends who've adopted children, and most states require prospective adoptive parents to meet several qualifications before the adoption is finalized. They often have to take classes on first aid, CPR, parenting skills, nutrition, and other essentials of raising an infant. Some would-be parents even have to pass tests. They also have to demonstrate to a social worker that they have a safe and healthy home in which to raise a child.

It's a good idea, of course, for the state to protect babies by making sure the adoptive parents are qualified. What's interesting to me, though, is that no biological parent has to take any classes or pass any tests. Anyone past the age of puberty can become a dad or a mom at any time—no matter what kind of a person he or she is. In order to drive a car or to own a gun or to leave the country, you must first be documented by the government. But to raise a human being from square one, no license is required.

In the grand scheme, that's a good thing. I don't want the government to decide who should be allowed to raise their own babies. But I do wish some parents took the job a little more seriously. So does God. He's spelled out several very specific instructions for parents in his Word. If your parents take God's Word seriously, then you've probably noticed that they try to follow these instructions. But that's not always an easy thing to do. Let's look at a few of God's requirements for parents.

LOVE GOD AND OTHERS

God's first instructions to parents are the two commands he gives to all of us:

> "'Love the Lord your God with all your heart and with all your soul and with all your strength and with all your mind'; and, 'Love your neighbor as yourself.'" (Luke 10:27)

Being a good parent starts with being in a right relationship with God the Father. That can only happen for those who've trusted in Jesus for the forgiveness of sin and for eternity in heaven with him. Even then, it's a challenge for believers to love God with our whole lives and to love our "neighbors" (everyone God brings into our path) as we do ourselves.

That doesn't mean all non-Christians are lousy parents. Unbelieving parents can be wise people and provide their kids with a good start in life. What they can't do, though, is point their kids to the Source of all wisdom by learning to live a Christlike life in front of their kids.

If you have Christian parents who really seem to want to live for God, then thank your Father in heaven for that gift. If not, then thank God that he provides "everything [you] need for life and godliness" (2 Peter 1:3).

HUSBANDS AND WIVES

God's next commands to parents don't have anything to do with their kids, either. God's instructions to moms deal with their role as wives to their husbands first—and vice versa for the men.

Wives, submit to your husbands as to the Lord. For the husband is the head of the wife as Christ is the head of the church, his body, of which he is the Savior. Now as the church submits to Christ, so also wives should submit to their husbands in everything. Husbands, love your wives, just as Christ loved the church and gave himself up for her. (Ephesians 5:22-25)

God cares deeply about how parents live together. In fact, God designed marriage as a picture of his enormous love for us in Jesus. Husbands are to give themselves to their wives unconditionally as Jesus did for all of us. And wives are to submit and give unconditional respect to their husbands as we (the church) are supposed to do with Jesus.

The way that works out in real life is often messy, complicated, and painful.

Following those commands is hard, no matter how you look at them. Still, those verses are part of God's instructions to parents. Good dads are learning how to love their wives without any strings attached. Good moms are learning how to give respect to their flawed husbands. By doing that, parents help their kids see God's plan for our eternity with him.

Does that mean that if your parents are divorced—or if one of them isn't obedient to these commands—then they can't be good parents? Not necessarily, but it's part of God's instructions to Christian men and women for a reason. It's God's plan for families, including your family.

If your parents are believers who are trying to follow those commands about being godly husbands and wives, then thank God that they are and for how their efforts are benefiting your life. If that's not the case in your home, then thank God that he provides for you as your eternal Father.

TEACH YOUR CHILDREN

Now we get around to some of the things God commands your parents to do in their relationship with you. And this is one of the biggies: Their job is to teach you about God and his Word.

Here's what God said to the Israelites after God promised to bless their nation as long as they followed him:

> Fix these words of mine in your hearts and minds; tie them as symbols on your hands and bind them on your foreheads. Teach them to your children, talking about them when you sit at home and when you walk along the road, when you lie down and when you get up. Write them on the doorframes of your houses and on your gates, so that your days

and the days of your children may be many in the land that the Lord swore to give your forefathers, as many as the days that the heavens are above the earth. (Deuteronomy 11:18-21)

The promise God made to Israel was conditional. "Keep following me," God said, "and I'll keep blessing you. Stop following me by ignoring the law or worshipping other gods, and I'll discipline you harshly." When God made that promise, he had the attention of an entire generation of Israelites. And God gave them the job of passing on that teaching to their kids.

Many generations of Israelites failed at that job. They didn't teach their children well, and their children ignored God. So God kept his promise and disciplined them by allowing other nations to defeat them. Eventually, another generation would come back to God and again be blessed by him. Inevitably, though, one generation would fail to teach the next, which would bring on more judgment and more pain.

We do NOT live under a conditional promise from God now. Those of us who've trusted in Jesus have our sins forgiven. We have a guaranteed home in heaven. Still, God wants parents to teach their kids about him. That's the job of moms and dads, to show their kids what it means to follow God and to help their kids understand God's Word.

To do that, parents have to talk about God and his Word all the time, as part of their regular lives—when sitting at home or in the car, when going to bed, and when getting up in the morning. God's idea was for parents to make his Word part of a family's ongoing conversation.

He says it again in Proverbs: "Train a child in the way he should go, and when he is old he will not turn from it" (Proverbs 22:6).

Then again in the New Testament: "Bring them up in the training and instruction of the Lord" (Ephesians 6:4).

It's a big job. If your parents are trying to obey God by teaching you his Word, then you can thank God for their willingness to do that.

DISCIPLINE YOUR KIDS

None of us likes being disciplined or punished. We don't like to be told "No." We don't like the pain of getting spanked when we're younger or getting grounded when we're older. We don't like to lose our access to the phone, Internet, video games, or car when Mom or Dad lowers the boom.

And as you may or may not know, most parents don't like to discipline their kids, either. It's not fun. In fact, it can feel downright ugly to enforce a rule or to come up with an appropriate punishment for bad behavior. So why do we do it?

There are two reasons. First, Christians do it because God's Word tells us to do it. Second, most parents (Christian or not) discipline their kids because it's understood in most parts of the world that kids need discipline in order to understand how best to live. Not disciplining our kids would be foolish, unwise, and potentially damaging.

Look at these proverbs from the Bible's key book of wisdom:

> He who spares the rod hates his son, but he who loves him is careful to discipline him. (Proverbs 13:24)

Discipline your son, for in that there is hope; do not be a willing party to his death. (Proverbs 19:18)

Those are the kinds of verses that keep parents up at night. *You mean, if I don't spank my son, then I hate him? If I don't discipline my teenager, then I'm actually participating in her destruction?*

God gives parents the huge responsibility to use painful consequences in their kids' lives to teach the difference between right and wrong and to help their kids learn to make good choices.

In the heat of the moment, it's really hard for kids to see discipline as an act of love. And, honestly, some parents take it too far. We can be too strict. We can cause too much hurt. But most parents discipline out of love and for the good of their kids. If yours do, then thank God for that. As we'll see later in this book, God also disciplines his children.

DADS: DON'T MAKE YOUR KIDS ANGRY

This last one is a toughie.

> Fathers, do not exasperate your children; instead, bring them up in the training and instruction of the Lord. (Ephesians 6:4)

> Fathers, do not embitter your children, or they will become discouraged. (Colossians 3:21)

Why do fathers have to be specifically commanded not to exasperate ("make furious") or embitter ("cause to be resentful") their kids? Part of the problem is that it's hard to know exactly what these two verses mean—and part of the problem is that so many dads disobey them. But the overall idea seems to echo that old Spider-Man philosophy: "With great power comes great responsibility."

In both passages the command follows an instruction to kids: "Children, obey your parents in everything, for this pleases the Lord" (Colossians 3:20). That command to you gives a lot of power to your parents—especially to your dad, the one who's usually assumed to be the ultimate authority in the family.

Paul seems to be warning dads that it's really easy to abuse their power. Whether it's by being unfair or too strict or hypocritical or hypercritical or stingy with their approval, dads have the power to make kids angry.

The big idea is that Dad is supposed to discipline with a spirit of love. He's supposed to love his wife as Jesus loves the church and to love his own kids as God loves him. If you're feeling resentful of your dad right now, then it would be easy for you to point out his failures in this area. If you're feeling a little more generous, then I hope you'll see what a tough job fatherhood is. God tells your dad, "Use your authority in your child's life to discipline—but don't misuse it and make him an angry person. Find the balance."

With the end of this chapter drawing near, you may be asking, *What's the point of discussing God's commands to parents?* Good question. First, I wanted to give you a little taste of what a hard job parenting is—especially for parents who are trying to do it according to God's plan. If your folks sometimes seem too preachy or too strict or too nagging, then it might be because they're trying to live up to a really high standard of parenthood.

Second, I don't think you can really build a wise relationship with someone until you know what his or her part in the relationship is supposed to be.

Third, I think it's only fair for you to understand how much God asks of your parents before we start talking about how much God asks from you in the parent-child relationship. It helps to know that both sides are called to do their part.

CHAPTER 4

WHAT GOD TELLS
KIDS TO DO

If you made it through the last chapter, then you saw that God expects (some would say "demands") quite a bit from parents. He instructs them to build good marriages, teach their children about the Bible, and find the balance between life-saving discipline and resentment-building abuse of authority. It's a tough job, and nobody's perfect at it.

The next question is, *What does God expect from kids?* The Bible was written long before the concept of a "teenager" existed. In the Jewish culture of New Testament times, kids moved into near-adulthood around the age of 13. In biblical times it would have been perfectly normal to find teenage girls married and having babies, as well as teenage guys having already invested a few years into a lifelong trade or career.

Obviously our culture today has wildly different expectations for people between the ages of 13 and 18. As Ms. Spears put it so eloquently a few years ago, "I'm not a girl, not yet a woman." These days, teenagers aren't usually treated as children, but they're still not given the rights and responsibilities of adults.

Some teenagers see the Bible's commands to "children" and assume they no longer apply to them. *After all, I'm not a kid*, they reason—mistakenly, as it turns out. Although I'd never call a teenage student a "child," God's Word teaches that we're all under someone's authority. When God gives instructions to children, God is talking directly to anyone still living at home and under his or her parents' authority. Until they've packed up their rooms and moved out, that includes even the older teenagers.

We shouldn't feel too badly about it. God refers to people of every age as his children. The Israelites are often called the "children of Israel." And the New Testament writers refer to adult men and women they care about as "dear children." So it's no insult to be called a child while you're still waiting for the right time to leave your parents' house and start living an independent life.

OBEY IS NOT A FOUR-LETTER WORD

And what does God ask of children? He makes one very specific command through the pen of the apostle Paul. Then he repeats it in another book of the Bible. Here are both versions:

> Children, obey your parents in the Lord, for this is right. "Honor your father and mother"—which is the first commandment with a promise— "that it may go well with you and

that you may enjoy long life on the earth." (Ephesians 6:1-3)

Children, obey your parents in everything, for this pleases the Lord. (Colossians 3:20)

Literally speaking, *obey* is a four-letter word. And I realize some people believe it's an uglier word than the ones that magically turn PG-rated movies into PG-13. In fact, I've heard people try to avoid using the word *obey* as if it were a swear word because they were afraid of making someone angry.

In our culture the idea of obedience really does offend some people. How dare we suggest that one person should have to do something that he or she doesn't want to do simply because someone in authority said so! Very few people like the idea of submitting to authority. We're very sensitive about who's allowed to tell us what to do—and who's *not*. Every sibling has spouted the words that are sung repeatedly in the *Malcolm in the Middle* theme song: "You're not the boss of me!"

Of course, saying those words implies that someone *is* the boss of me. For some students I've met, that idea is just too much to take. Even when they agree with their parents' instructions, they resent doing what they're told. For them, obedience actually causes emotional pain.

But this idea of being under the authority of other humans is how God designed the world to work—and God's design always makes sense. Let's break down what God's asking us to do exactly—and work at understanding why.

WE OBEY GOD FIRST

Notice, first of all, that this obedience thing is a command from God. The biggest problem with not obeying Mom and Dad isn't that we're being "bad" to them. The biggest problem is that we're disobeying God. He's the one telling us to obey our parents.

I don't know about you, but that helps me in a big way. Why? Because I know without a doubt that God loves me deeply. Nobody else has given a son to die for me. Nobody else has forgiven all my sins (including all the times I disobeyed my parents). Nobody will ever love me the way God does. Because of all that God's done for me, it's easier for me to obey him.

I think that's what "obey your parents in the Lord" means. It doesn't mean we have to obey only those parents who are "in the Lord." It means we obey our parents because *we're* "in the Lord"— because we do it for God.

OBEYING OUR PARENTS MAKES GOD HAPPY

In Ephesians 6, Paul says we obey Mom and Dad because it's "right." In Colossians 3, he tells us it "pleases the Lord." That also helps me some. I don't obey just because "God said so." I obey because it actually makes God happy. It pleases him. I don't know of too many things I can do all by myself to please the God of the universe. It would be an honor to do that, though, and this is one way that I can.

It reminds me of that verse in Hebrews that says, "Without faith it is impossible to please God" (11:6). Obeying your parents is a way to please God because it's an act of faith. Sometimes we just don't want to obey our parents. At other times it doesn't seem to make sense to obey them. But when we choose to do it anyway, we're demonstrating that we actually believe God is trustworthy.

"I think my parents are wrong"—or too strict or hurtful or power-tripping— "but I love God. I have to believe God is right when he tells me to obey them. I'll take God's Word for it. I'll trust him, even if I can't see that my parents deserve it." That's faith—and God enjoys seeing it grow in you.

OBEYING OUR PARENTS IS NOT MERIT-BASED

Just like every child, every parent fails sometimes. While most parents love their kids deeply all the time, they can still be selfish, sinful, hurtful, unkind, neglectful, and uncaring. Some parents are better than others at giving love and attention to their kids. What if yours will never be poster-worthy? Does that give you an out on the whole obedience thing?

Not so much. God's command to obey is unconditional. God doesn't include any stipulations regarding whether or not your parents are believers, are kind, or are having a bad day (or decade). He doesn't even qualify it by saying, "Obey just as long as you believe your parents are at least trying to do what's right." Knowing that God offers no exceptions makes it a little easier for me to obey.

Even though it's hard to obey authorities who don't earn my respect, my obedience ultimately has nothing to do with them. It's all about my love for God. In the big picture, it doesn't really matter who my mom and dad are as people.

Okay, there is one exception. I sometimes receive e-mails from students asking about parents who tell them to do wrong things. Sinful things. Things that go against what God has told them to do. In that case I believe God's Word is clear that we must obey him first because we are "in the Lord." So that might give you an out if your parents ask you to lie, steal, or ignore God's

Word in other ways. Honestly, though, those situations are pretty rare.

So God's Word is pretty definite about this obedience thing. We'll wrestle a little more with the specifics of getting along with parents later in this book. But in the next chapter, we'll take a quick look at the other half of these commands to "children."

CHAPTER 4
WHAT GOD TELLS KIDS TO DO

CHAPTER 5
WISE AND STUBBORN HONOR

It was 7:53 p.m., and we were locked out of the house. But *The A-Team* was going to start in seven minutes!

For my brothers and me, Tuesday night was big church night. I had junior high Bible study, and my brothers had church scouts (or something like that). After church we'd catch a ride home with a family friend and then race into the house to watch our all-time favorite TV show.

For my parents, Tuesday night was free time. I'm not sure what they did while we were gone. But on this particular night, they weren't home when we got there. A note taped to the front door read—

> Mark,
> We'll be back late. Be sure to feed Jonathan's rabbit while you wait.
> Love,
> Mom and Dad

I was infuriated! Didn't they know that Mr. T and *The A-Team* were starting soon? How could they leave us out in the cold while they pranced around town like childless married people?

I ripped the note off the door and sat down in the yard. Josh, Jeremy, and Jonathan joined me. All my dad seemed to care about was that we feed Jonathan's rabbit—which Jonathan had done before we left!

I was very upset at my parents. My brothers were mad, too. Josh and Jeremy had homework to do; Jonathan was just mad because we were.

Now it was 8:30 p.m., and *The A-Team*, the coolest show on earth, was half over.

I picked up a baseball bat and started whacking a tree. How could my parents be so rude? Josh and Jeremy were looking all around the house for an

open door or window. Everything was locked tight.

Finally, at 9:30 p.m., my parents pulled into the drive. Four angry Matlock boys rushed out to jump them. As the four of us expressed our displeasure in no uncertain terms, my dad asked me if I'd fed the rabbit. I told him no, and then I reminded him that Jonathan had fed it *before* we went to church.

My dad walked us over to the rabbit food. There, taped to the bag, was the key to the house.

"What did you want me to do, Mark?" my father asked in a Mike Brady-like tone. "Did you want me to leave a note that said the key was taped to the rabbit food so anyone who read the note could find it?"

If I'd honored my dad, my evening would have been much happier. Instead, I was a fool worthy of Mr. T's pity. (See, that's a joke for people who've seen *The A-Team*. Mr. T was always saying, "I pity the fool!" I'm not really sure why, now that I think about it. I just knew he was cool.)

Instead of honoring my dad by following his instructions, I jumped to the conclusion that he just didn't get it. He didn't understand that the rabbit had already been fed. So I'd decided his instruction was worthless. But if I'd stopped to remember that Dad usually did a good job of providing for us and giving us worthwhile direction, I would have honored him by honoring his note. And that literally would have been the key to my *A-Team* happiness.

We saw in the last chapter that the fifth of the top Ten Commandments was the "first with a promise." Here it is from Exodus 20:12: "Honor your father and your mother, so that you may live long in the land the Lord your God is giving you." Since Paul repeats it in Ephesians 6:1-3 and Solomon emphasizes it in Proverbs, we still hold on to the idea that honoring our parents leads to longer, wiser living.

That makes sense, doesn't it? I'm not saying parents are always right. In fact, sometimes they can be selfish, too strict, or too lenient. So what? What other two people in the universe have made it their jobs to love you, take care of you, and invest their lives in you for your own good? That's what parents do.

Since they've been doing it for so long, we sometimes take their investment for granted. It's human nature for us to ignore the things they do right and with good motives 80 percent of the time (or more!) and to be on the lookout for anything they might screw up instead. To continue to honor your mom and dad (even when you don't understand where they're coming from) takes wisdom and a stubborn refusal to give in to the temptation to dishonor them.

HOW TO HONOR YOUR PARENTS

Let's say you've embraced the idea that honoring your parents makes sense because God commands it—and because it leads to a longer and more enjoyable life. What does it *mean* to honor your parents? Let's get some wise hints from Proverbs.

PAY ATTENTION WHEN THEY TALK

Listen, my son, to your father's instruction and do not forsake your mother's teaching. (Proverbs 1:8)

Listen, my sons, to a father's instruction; pay attention and gain understanding. (Proverbs 4:1)

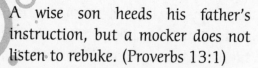

A wise son heeds his father's instruction, but a mocker does not listen to rebuke. (Proverbs 13:1)

Listen to your father, who gave you life, and do not despise your mother when she is old. (Proverbs 23:22)

I would add to that last one that it's probably better not to mention to your mother that she's old. But that's beside the point. Did you notice a theme in those four verses?

Solomon writes many of his proverbs from the perspective of a dad offering urgent and essential advice to his sons. He's desperate to help them learn from his experience and wisdom. He wants to make sure they don't miss out on living lives that really matter. But all he can do is beg them to pay attention to him (and to their moms). No parents can force their child to really listen to their directions, their point of view, or their take on life, which they've developed over many years. In the end, it's up to the children to decide whether or not to tune in to Radio Dad and KMOM.

Tuning in. Paying attention. Making sure you *get* what your parents say. That's one way to honor your parents.

Before we look at the next way, I want you to notice something else in Proverbs. Look at where Solomon says he got the idea to make "getting wisdom" a high priority in his life:

> When I was a boy in my father's house, still tender, and an only child of my mother, he taught me and said, "Lay hold of my words with all your heart; keep my commands and you will live. Get wisdom, get understanding; do not forget my words or swerve from them." (Proverbs 4:3-5)

Solomon honored his father, King David, by paying attention to him. That act of honoring his dad resulted in Solomon knowing exactly what he needed later on when God came to him and said, "I'll give you anything you want. What'll it be?" Solomon's answer: wisdom. He'd kept his dad's instructions close to his heart. So when the time came for a potentially life-changing decision, Solomon knew what to do.

GIVE RESPECT

Wait, you say, I can see why Solomon's sons (and daughters) honored their dad and listened to him. And I can see why Solomon honored his dad, King David. Both those men were wise, powerful, and God-fearing. Together, they wrote or were the subject of a huge chunk of Scripture. But my dad and mom are no King David or Solomon. They're just average people. Why should I care so much about honoring them?

Thanks for allowing me to put that question in your mouth so I can give you this answer. One of the big principles of Scripture is that we're to give respect to people in positions of authority—not based on their worthiness, but based on how they got there.

Look at this:

> Everyone must submit himself to the governing authorities, for there is no authority except that which God has established. The authorities that exist have been established by God. (Romans 13:1)

That's a difficult concept to wrap your mind around. God has established not only the institution of authority, but also every position of authority from the President of the United States on down to your parents. No matter who occupies the position, she deserves respect because she occupies a position established by God.

What does it mean to give respect? It's respectful to respond when someone talks to you; to control your volume and your attitude—even when you're hungry or tired or stressed; and to respond politely even when others aren't polite to you. Respect doesn't necessarily mean admitting that the other person is right or pretending that you like how the person is acting. Respect is simply acknowledging with your words and actions that the other person outranks you—or that another person has a dignity that even he may not be aware of.

LIVE WISELY

Your parents care very deeply about how you turn out. It's not enough for them to know that you're healthy and well provided for. They also want you to be a good person—a person of integrity, respectability, and wisdom.

Look at these words from Solomon's book:

> The father of a righteous man has great joy; he who has a wise son delights in him. May your father and mother be glad; may she who gave you birth rejoice! (Proverbs 23:24-25)

> A wise son brings joy to his father, but a foolish son grief to his mother. (Proverbs 10:1)

The fact that you're reading this book and trying to become a wiser person is, in a way, an act of honoring your parents. Searching for wisdom in any area of life is a way of honoring your parents. Trying hard to follow Jesus by making choices that honor God at school, at church, at home, and in the deep privacy of your own mind—*that's* honoring your parents.

Even if your folks don't seem to notice or care how you live, these verses confirm that your parents will be honored if you learn to live wisely, if you become a man or woman of integrity, if you follow after God. Becoming an honorable person honors your parents.

We could fill many chapters with ideas for how to honor your mom and dad, but you can use God's wisdom to search those out on your own. Let's move on and tackle some of the harder questions that teenagers and their parents face—such as how to get along with each other when conflict arises.

CHAPTER 6

INTERVIEWING YOUR PARENTS

You might assume you know everything there is to know about your parents. After all, you've lived with them (or at least one of them) for more than a dozen years now, maybe longer. You might be surprised, then, to learn there's a whole lot more to your mom and dad than you know. Things you have no clue about. Things that may completely change the way you think about them. I'm still discovering new things about my parents all these years since I moved out of their place—things that definitely would have changed the way I thought about them back in my occasionally heated teenage years.

One way to honor your parents (or anyone else) is to take an interest in them as people—find out what makes them the way they are. The more you know about your parents, the less likely it is that you'll continue to think of them as walking cash machines, dinner preparers, fun ruiners, or your personal drivers. Turn your parents into real (or more real), three-dimensional people by taking some time to interview them. Record the audio, make a video, or write a short bio for each of them.

The project will take some work on your part, but you might be surprised by what you learn. Did your mom ever work as a trapeze artist in the circus? Was your dad in the Russian mafia? How will you know if you don't ask? Even if you don't uncover any sensational or shocking history, you still might be stunned by how normal your mom and dad were as kids. And you'll definitely be amazed by how honored your parents will feel that you took the time to ask.

Here are 25 questions to get you started in your interview. But don't let my suggestions confine you. Get creative. Be a good journalist and follow up interesting answers with additional questions. Do your best Matt Lauer impersonation. Don't let your parents off the hook until you really understand what they're saying—or until they start to cry.

1. What's one of your earliest memories?

2. Which of your siblings were you closest to? Why?

3. What were some of your folks' strengths and weaknesses as parents?

4. Did you worry much about money when you were a kid? Did you think of your family as rich or poor—or did you not think about it at all?

5. What were some of your favorite things to do with your family?

6. What was your favorite vacation you took together?

7. What were your best and worst subjects in school?

8. What's one of your most embar-rassing moments?

9. What were your favorite TV shows, movies, and books? How did your parents feel about those choices?

10. What did you think about Jesus when you were a kid? How did your feelings about him change as you got older?

11. How old were you when you first started using the Internet or got an e-mail address?

12. When you were a teenager, did you have a lot of crushes? Did you act on them very often? Did you date very much?

13. Would you say you were popular in high school? If so, what kinds of pressures did that create? If not, did that bother you?

14. Who were your best friends in high school? Which was the funny

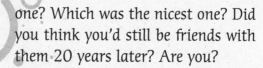

one? Which was the nicest one? Did you think you'd still be friends with them 20 years later? Are you?

15. Were you athletic? What were your favorite sports to play? Are you more or less competitive now than you were then?

16. If you could change one or two of the choices you made when you were in middle school or high school, would you? If so, which ones would you change and why?

17. Did your parents get mad at you very often? Did you think they were too strict?

18. If you could have changed one thing about how your parents dealt with you, what would it be?

19. When did you first meet Mom/ Dad? What attracted you to her/ him? How long did it take before you started dating? At the time did you ever imagine you'd end up together?

20. What's the farthest you've traveled from home? How many other states or countries have you been to? If you could visit any place in the world, where would you go?

21. What's been your best achievement in life so far?

22. When you were a kid, who were your heroes? Do you have any heroes today?

23. What were your best and worst jobs ever? Do you like the job you have now? If you could do any kind of job in the world, what would you pick? Why?

24. What's the hardest part of making a marriage work? What's the best part?

25. What surprised you about being a parent? What are the best and worst parts of that job for you?

CHAPTER 7

WHY PARENTS AND TEENAGERS FIGHT

You may be surprised to find this chapter in the middle of the book instead of the beginning. This topic may be the reason you picked up the book in the first place. If so, then you're probably bugged by all these chapters about what parents are supposed to do, how our job is to obey and honor them, and how we can better understand them.

You want to get down to the nitty-gritty. You want me to tell you how you can get your folks to back off, to give you a little more space, to treat you like a young adult instead of a child. Or perhaps you're coming to this book from a different perspective: You're hoping I can tell you how to get your folks to like you more, to spend more time with you, to be prouder of you.

I assure you, you're not the only one struggling with these issues. Students ask me about them all the time. And I'll tell you what I tell them: God's Word offers lots of wisdom when it comes to easing tensions between parent and child.

Before we get to that, though, let me give you the punch line to this chapter right up front. At the end of the day, you can't get your parents to do anything at all. You can't make them give you more space. You can't force them to give you their approval. The bottom line is this: You can't control how anyone treats you—and that includes your parents.

If that seems like a depressing thought, consider this one: Your parents have the same problem with you. If I were to write a parents' version of this book, then the punch line for the parents' chapter would say, "Guess what? You can't control your teenagers anymore. You can't make them less distant. You can't force them to take more responsibility in their lives. You can't make them try harder or study more or be nicer to their siblings."

And that's partly why parents and teenagers get so angry with each other. Your relationship has undergone some drastic changes in the last 10 years or so.

BUILT TO GET ALONG

Have you ever watched new parents with a baby? It's as if they're saying things such as, "Why won't he stop crying? What can we do to make him happy? Hey, Baby, here's some food. Here's some milk. Are you dirty? Let me change your diaper. Are you sleepy? I'll rock you in my arms. I'll do anything to make sure you're okay."

When you and your parents started your lives together, you could make each other do most of the things you wanted. From day one all you had to do was cry, and then Mom or Dad would come running to fix the problem. Their job was to keep you happy. In many ways babies are little dictators, and parents are their loyal, loving subjects.

Yet when the situation called for it, the roles could be reversed. When you were a child, your parents could pretty much make you do whatever they wanted. If you started to do something that was unsafe or too messy or even just inconvenient, they could stop you. They could pick you up and move you wherever they wanted you to be. They could hold your little hand and put it where it needed to go. They could change your outfit to whatever they thought was best for the day. When it was time to go somewhere, they just grabbed you and off you went.

As you got older, though, things started changing. Over time your parents started letting you make more of your

own decisions. You, in turn, started asking them to do fewer things for you. You and your parents likely clashed over differing wants and expectations when you were a toddler—and on up through grade school. But if your folks were obeying God by using the right kind of discipline, then you probably learned to respect their boundaries. You figured out that they weren't going to let you do whatever you wanted to do all the time. And they figured out that you were capable of doing things for yourself.

The relationship worked well through fifth grade or so partly because God designed you and your parents with some really helpful relationship instincts. By nature even really selfish parents want their kids to enjoy life, to learn skills that will help them live wisely, and to be well provided for. And kids, by nature, want to know that mom and dad love them, are proud of them, and will be there for them.

That's why, generally speaking, kids through elementary age tend to get along with their moms and dads. Even though there are incidents of childish rebellion or parental neglect, everyone more or less finds a way to coexist. Many families actually thrive during the grade-school years.

WHY AM I NOT IN CHARGE?

But all of those crazy puberty hormones have a way of scrambling everything. Before we get into that, though, let me emphasize that most teenagers and their parents get along really well—most of the time. A recent MTV survey asked 13-to-24 year olds what makes them happy. The number one response was "spending time with my family." So, contrary to popular stereotypes,

not every teenager-parent relationship plays out like a WWE cage match.

Of course most parents and teenagers do go at it sometimes. And those conflicts can be traced to the changes that are taking place inside of you. The more you change—physically, emotionally, and intellectually—the more your relationship with your folks also changes.

Puberty rewires your system and your priorities. As a result, you start to care more about what your friends think than you do about what your parents think. That makes you less motivated to smooth things over when Mom and Dad want you to do something you don't want to do—or want you to stop doing something you really want to do. A few years earlier, even though you may not have liked the situation any better, the back part of your brain would have said, *My parents are the most important people in the world to me, so I'd better work this out.* But now the back of your brain is starting to say (or yell), *I've got all kinds of potentially valuable relationships now, and I'll eventually be leaving this joint anyway. Maybe I should risk pushing harder for what I want this time.*

On the other side of the conflict, it's likely that your parents will be caught off guard by your dwindling interest in keeping them happy. Suddenly, you start to challenge the value of their decisions. You question their logic. Your responses begin to imply thoughts and feelings such as *Why?* or *What's the big deal?* or *Maybe you're not as smart as I thought you were.*

The problem is, your parents still have a job to do. God still tells them to point you in the right direction, to discipline you when you sin, and to keep you from danger. Even unbelieving parents

understand that those things are still part of their job. But their job has become harder because you're no longer willing to give them the benefit of the doubt when they offer advice or instruction.

That change in attitude makes some parents really angry. Some respond by becoming stricter in an effort to control teenagers who seem to want to break free at every opportunity. Others, afraid of losing their kids' friendship, turn into permissive puppy dogs who let their kids get away with almost anything. Most parents try to find a balance between ruling with an iron fist and giving up completely. They really want to help their teenage sons and daughters gain more independence—without making too many unwise choices.

Along the way, though, every parent occasionally falls off the balance beam in one direction or the other. And all the students I've met struggle with what it means to honor and obey their moms and dads when they *know* they're ready to live life their own way.

Now that we've broken down one source of parent-teenager conflict, let's talk about what you can do about it. Remember, you can't change your parents, but that doesn't mean you're powerless. You have options for repairing the rough parts of your relationship with your parents.

CHAPTER 8
TRUE INDEPENDENCE

said it before, and I'll say it again: You can't control the way your parents respond to you. No matter what strategy you choose for dealing with your parents—whether it's complete rebellion, perfect obedience, or something in between—there's no guarantee you'll get the results you hope for. Ultimately, the way your parents respond to you is a matter between them and God.

That's why the apostle Paul wrote, "If it is possible, as far as it depends on you, live at peace with everyone" (Romans 12:18). God understands that when it comes to making peace with someone, you can do only *your* part. He doesn't hold you responsible for the other person's reaction to you—even when that other person is your parent.

BREAKING FREE WITHIN YOUR HEART

The wisest strategy for dealing with your parents, then, is to become so independent of them that it no longer matters who they are or how they treat you. The best way to make peace with your mom and dad—and still walk in a right relationship with them—is to unhook the emotional baggage that weighs down your interactions with them.

Don't misunderstand me. I'm not suggesting you turn off your emotions or become disrespectful and detached. My point is that God is beginning to call you to relate to your parents as simply the people he loves, not as the people who run your life. Look at Jesus' words:

> Anyone who loves his father or mother more than me is not worthy of me; anyone who loves his son or daughter more than me is not

worthy of me; and anyone who does not take his cross and follow me is not worthy of me. Whoever finds his life will lose it, and whoever loses his life for my sake will find it. (Matthew 10:37-39)

Here's the radical idea: You can be truly independent of your parents right now, today, at this very moment. You don't have to wait until you move out or go away to college to become independent of them—in your heart. You *do* have to wait for those things to happen before you can stop living by your parents' rules, but you don't have to wait to start living on your own emotionally and spiritually.

How do you become independent of your parents? You declare your intention to follow Jesus with your whole self. You declare your allegiance to him *above* all else. You deny yourself, take up your cross, and head out on his path. Did you catch what Jesus said about your parents in the above Scripture passage? You might want to read it again.

If you care more about your parents than you care about Jesus, then you're not worthy of him. The same goes for them in relation to you. When you can honestly say you care more about Jesus than you do about your folks, you'll know you're independent of them. And here's the kicker: You'll be able to love, obey, and honor them with a freedom and a willingness you've never had before.

It will still be your job to give your parents respect and honor. It will still be your job to obey them. But you can remove the personal drama from your job. You'll obey your parents because that's what Jesus did—and it's what he tells you to do. It doesn't matter if your parents are awesome or terrible. You obey them for Jesus. You treat them

respectfully for his sake. They may or may not deserve your respect, but that's beside the point. You serve Jesus.

JESUS' PARENTS

We mentioned earlier that Jesus set an example of obedience for us in his relationship with his parents. All three of them.

First of all, Jesus is God's Son. We can learn some things about how to treat our dads from Jesus' relationship with God the Father, although it's obviously not a perfect comparison. One of the first clues we find in Scripture regarding the relationship between Jesus and God is in Matthew 3. After Jesus' baptism, God could be heard saying, "This is my Son, whom I love; with him I am well pleased" (verse 17). Most of us would love to hear such words from our dads.

In return Jesus gave God the Father tons of respect. He made it clear that he came to earth in obedience to his Father. He repeatedly said that his words came from the Father. He was careful to publicly thank the Father for every gift, giving God props in the presence of others. Jesus was honest with the Father about not wanting to die on the cross—and then he submitted to the Father's will.

Again, Jesus' relationship with his Father is different from our relationships with our human fathers. Obviously, our dads aren't God. Still, God tells us to honor, respect, obey, and submit to our dads.

We're not told very much about Jesus' relationship with his dad, Joseph. Most scholars assume Joseph died between the time Jesus was 12 and 30 years old. Jesus did go into the family business of carpentry for a time, so we might assume that he was willing to learn those skills from his dad, that he was teachable. We've already seen in an earlier chapter of this book that God calls us to be teachable toward our parents: "Listen, my sons, to a father's instruction; pay attention and gain understanding" (Proverbs 4:1).

Jesus' relationship with Mary might be easier for us to relate to. We see both positive and strained moments between Jesus and his honorable-but-imperfect human mom. His first miracle comes about as an act of honoring and obeying his mother, even though he told her, "Dear woman, why do you involve me? My time has not yet come" (John 2:4). And then he did what she asked.

Later, though, Jesus made the point that his first allegiance was not to his mother (or his brothers). When told his family was waiting for him apart from the crowd he was teaching, Jesus said that all who do God's will are his mothers and brothers—his true family (Matthew 12:46-50). That's an idea we have to hold on to as well. Jesus took responsibility for his mom even as he was hanging on the cross—asking John to take care of her, as a good son should (John 19:26-27). But Jesus served God and his family in the church first and above all else.

Now let's get really practical. What's it look like to get along with your parents when you're living as a Jesus-follower? That's what we'll tackle in the next chapter.

CHAPTER 9
THE FINE ART OF PARENTAL NEGOTIATION

Oh, yes, there will be conflict. There will be disagreements over the best course of action, the best outfit to wear, the best curfew time, the right amount of butter for those pancakes, and even the right friends to hang out with. Those moments will come.

In the last chapter, we introduced a new way of thinking about our parents: They shouldn't matter to us nearly as much as following Jesus matters to us. We talked about how that perspective gives us the freedom to remove some of the emotion from our conflicts with our parents.

A few chapters before that, we talked about another big idea—that God works in our lives through various positions of authority. That even when someone in authority is wrong, we can choose to believe God is working for our good and directing our lives through that set of circumstances. In other words, God is the one who ultimately allows us to be restricted from wearing a certain top, hanging out with a certain guy, or eating a seventh slice of pizza. Our parents are simply the people God uses to direct us. Therefore, our relationship is with—and our responses are to—God.

Putting those two big ideas together, we can talk about some strategies for resolving conflict with parents. Be warned: Actually living this way takes a lot of maturity. It's much easier to get hacked off at your mom for not letting you do something—or for punishing you too harshly—than it is to say, "For some reason, God is using my mom to direct my life in this way."

Still, this is the path of wisdom. Why? Let's get more specific.

THE TOTAL HONESTY STRATEGY

God hates lying. I mean, he really, really hates it. If you don't believe me, take a gander at Proverbs 6:16-19. It's a list of seven things God hates (not dislikes, but hates!). And lying makes the list twice! Clearly, lying is a sin and it's wrong.

I've never understood why some Christian students who seem to be serious about following Jesus believe it's acceptable and normal to lie to their parents. You can't lie to your mom or dad and still be okay with God. You have to confess your untruth as a sin—to God and to your parents—and you have to make it right. Otherwise, you're wrong.

I know it's hard to understand that because lying to parents has become so common today. Many students put it in the same category as speeding—something everyone does without a second thought. But that's not okay. Remember, this goes beyond your relationship with your parents. This is about following Jesus. And Jesus hates it when we lie to anybody. Period.

A better strategy can be found 180 degrees from lying. I'm talking about complete openness and honesty.

Tell your parents the truth about everything, all the time, no matter what. That doesn't mean you shouldn't have your own private thoughts or you shouldn't ever hold anything in confidence from your folks. It does mean that telling them way more than you'd prefer to tell will help you get more freedom from them down the road.

So, volunteer things like where you went after school, who you were with, what you did, and when you got home. Without getting angry, be respectfully honest with them regarding how you feel about some of their rules—then obey them anyway. When you get in trouble at school, come straight home and tell your folks what happened and why. They might punish you, but they'll also start to see that you're not keeping things from them.

Here's a secret about parents I'm probably not supposed to tell you: When your parents begin to wonder if you're telling the truth or hiding something, that's when they ask the most questions and begin to clamp down on you. When they see that you always come clean—even when it might cost you something—they'll be much more likely to let you go further on your own.

Complete honesty is the best way to gain more trust, more freedom, and more respect from your parents. Being honest in all situations is the right thing to do. It's what Jesus-followers do. It also happens to be the way to get along best with your mom and dad.

The principle is captured in Proverbs 16:13 (if you think of your parents—your authority—as kingly rulers): "Kings take pleasure in honest lips; they value a man who speaks the truth."

THE OWN-YOUR-PART STRATEGY

For those who've made a habit of lying, this might take some work. Some may even have to learn to start telling themselves the truth. Look at what Solomon's dad, David, wrote in Psalm 51:6—"Surely you desire truth in the inner parts; you teach me wisdom in the inmost place."

When students talk to me about an ongoing battle with their parents, I ask, "What percentage of this fight would you say is your problem, and what percentage is your parents' problem?" Guess what? Most students admit that they know the problem is more than half theirs, often putting the figure in the neighborhood of 70 percent! Just thinking about the question forces them to be honest in their "inner parts."

If you're a Jesus-follower who has an ongoing negative issue with your parents, then ask yourself that question. Then, whatever you believe your percentage is, take that to Jesus and ask him to help you deal with it. Ask him to help you obey and honor him in the matter, then make some choices to clear up your part of the problem.

Next—and this is the harder part—talk to your parents about your estimated percentages. Say something like, "Mom, I believe 60 percent of this issue we've been having is my problem. I'm trying to clear that up between God and me and do the right thing. I still don't agree with your 40 percent, but I've decided to obey and honor your direction anyway."

Talk about honesty! And now I'll be honest with you: Not all parents will appreciate that approach, but they'll have to acknowledge that you're being honest and that you're taking the idea of following Jesus seriously. What will come from that? More trust. More freedom. And less friction with the folks.

THE ASK-FOR-ADVICE STRATEGY

Speaking from experience, I can tell you that parents are suckers for this one. Again, though, the point of these strategies isn't to dupe Mom and Dad. As a Jesus-follower you're not trying to get away with doing anything wrong. But as a teenager, you're trying to get more freedom and respect from your parents. This is a good way to do that—and it's also a great way to get wisdom.

In short, the strategy is this: Ask for advice. You have decisions to make. You have problems with friends or sports or school. Make a point of asking your mom or dad for their wisdom and insight once in a while.

Proverbs again: "Plans fail for lack of counsel, but with many advisers they succeed" (15:22). So not only will asking your folks for counsel get them on your side, but they might also have

some ideas you haven't thought of yet. Getting advice from new sources is a great way to figure out a problem. It never hurts to ask.

THE MAKE-YOUR-CASE-AND-LET-IT-GO STRATEGY

This strategy comes into play anytime you deal with an authority figure who's deciding against your wishes on an issue. In other words, this is worth practicing with your parents now so you'll have it in your strategy bag when you deal with other authority figures later on.

Sometimes your parents will make a decision that just seems wrong, unfair, unwise, or maybe even a little crazy. When that happens, you have several options—especially if you're not worried about following Jesus. You could defy them and do what you want. You could deceive them and do what you want. You could blow up in explosive anger, swear, slam doors, and try to bully them into backing down. Or you could try to manipulate them with tears, pouting, withholding your time and attention, or saying hurtful things to them.

As a Jesus-follower, you have to take those options off your menu. What's left? Making your case. That involves a little preparation and then "approaching the king" with humility. Figure out ahead of time what points you want to make. Ask for an opportunity to talk about the issue. Use a respectful voice and respectful words. Say right up front that you'll honor whatever decision is made.

Because you believe that God is ultimately the one who controls your life, even this strategy isn't really about your parents. It's about trusting God to give you what he thinks is best. After all, "The king's heart is in the hand of the Lord; he directs it like a watercourse wherever he pleases" (Proverbs 21:1).

You'd be surprised how often this approach works when it comes to modifying a decision from parents— or from anyone in authority. King David practiced this approach with God the Father in the midst of a very serious matter. David had lusted for Bathsheba, a married woman...he had sex with her...he got her pregnant...he had her husband killed...and then he married her. David's actions were evil in every sense of the word, yet David ignored them. God, however, didn't. God revealed to David that his and Bathsheba's baby would die.

David was heartsick. He made his case before God, and he became very emotional. Here's the passage from 2 Samuel 12:

> David pleaded with God for the child. He fasted and went into his house and spent the nights lying on the ground. The elders of his household

stood beside him to get him up from the ground, but he refused, and he would not eat any food with them. (vv. 16-17)

It's an extreme example, but do you see what David did? Fasting and prayer are very respectful ways of getting God's attention and letting him know you're serious. David acknowledged God's power to change his mind and heal the child. David humbled himself dramatically and made his request.

Yet God still said no. The baby died. And David's servants were afraid to tell David the news because they thought he might hurt himself (or them!). Instead:

David got up from the ground. After he had washed, put on lotions and changed his clothes, he went into the house of the Lord and worshiped. Then he went to his own house, and

at his request they served him food, and he ate.

His servants asked him, "Why are you acting this way? While the child was alive, you fasted and wept, but now that the child is dead, you get up and eat!"

He answered, "While the child was still alive, I fasted and wept. I thought, 'Who knows? The Lord may be gracious to me and let the child live.' But now that he is dead, why should I fast? Can I bring him back again?" (vv. 20-23)

David made his request; but once he knew God's decision was final, he let it go. That's a key for you, too, in making your case with your parents. Once they're clear that the decision is final, it's time for you to let it go and accept that as God's direction for your life.

CHAPTER 10
MINISTER TO MY PARENTS?

Want to take your relationship with your parents to a completely different level? Want to move beyond "obey and honor"? Want to advance past strategies for merely getting along with your folks? Try this: Embrace your relationship with your parents as a personal ministry.

Jesus calls us to represent him to everyone we interact with—siblings, friends, classmates, the guy in the drive-through window, and even our parents. If you're serious about that call, you'll say to yourself, *While I'm under my mom and dad's authority, I'm going to make a difference in their lives. I'm not content with merely surviving this relationship until I can leave home. I'm going to find ways to be a positive influence in my parents' lives.*

I'm not suggesting that you should try to be something unhealthy to your parents. Your job isn't to be their teacher or counselor. You're not called to fix their problems. Instead, I'm suggesting that you aim for a standard beyond what your mom and dad expect of you. Ask yourself, *What would Jesus do if he were my parents' child?*

MINISTRY OPPORTUNITIES

Ministering to the people in our lives means using our time to build relationships that will benefit them. That kind of ministry involves a lot of prayer and a willingness to ask yourself some relevant questions.

Here are a few examples:

- What could I say right now that would encourage my parent(s)?

- How could I help in a way that might take some pressure off them?

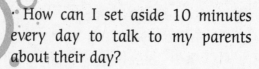

· How can I set aside 10 minutes every day to talk to my parents about their day?

· Is there something I could pick up for them at the store, the drive-through, or the coffee shop that might brighten their day a little?

· Could I take something off their plate full of responsibilities so they can spend quality time together or with a good friend?

· Am I willing to be tuned into my parents as people made in the image of God when we're together?

You'd be amazed what a difference you can make in someone's life simply by being available to be used by God as a minister of Jesus. Your parents are the perfect people to practice on as you begin to build this into your lifestyle.

HOW TO PRAY FOR YOUR PARENTS

Every relationship can be improved if you're willing to pray for the other person. If you already get along well with someone, then praying can deepen your understanding of him and increase your compassion for him. If you've been in conflict with the person, then praying can be difficult. If you believe the person has really wronged you, then praying can be even harder. But it can—and should—be done, especially in a relationship as important as the one you have with your parents.

Take some time to pray for your mom and dad on a regular basis. That in itself is a gift and an act of kindness. But it's more than that. Prayer actually changes the universe as God draws near to us in response to our drawing near to him.

Here are a few things you could pray for your parents, but don't limit yourself to just this list. Allow God's Spirit to prompt you to pray for your folks as they need it most.

· If one or both (or all) of your parents aren't believers, then pray that they'd come to know God as Father through faith in Jesus as their Savior.

· If your parents are believers, then ask God to help them love him more, trust him more, and want him more.

· Ask God to give your folks wisdom to be good parents to you every day, to help them know how much freedom to give you and what restrictions to put on you.

· Ask God to give your parents a strong, stable, and healthy marriage. Ask God to help your dad love his wife as Jesus loved the church. Ask God to help your mom obey the New Testament commands for wives. Ask

God to help your parents grow to like each other more all the time. Ask God to give them a healthy and pure physical relationship. Ask God to help them forgive and be patient with each other.

· Ask God to help your parents find ways to enjoy their work, to be satisfied in it, and to do it well. Ask God to help them learn to use their money wisely.

· Ask God to give them the wisdom to relate to their own parents.

· If your folks are believers, ask that the fruit of the Spirit from Galatians 5:22-23—love, joy, peace, patience, kindness, goodness, faithfulness, gentleness, and self-control—would become more obvious in their lives.

· Ask God to give your parents wisdom regarding any big decisions they're facing (job changes, moves, going back to school, ministry opportunities).

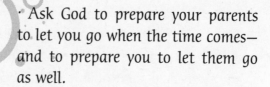

· Ask God to prepare your parents to let you go when the time comes—and to prepare you to let them go as well.

· Make it a point to regularly give God thanks for any of your parents' good qualities. Ask God to help you to grow in those same qualities.

· Ask God to help you encourage your parents by learning to live wisely in your personal life.

CHAPTER 11

WRITE A RELATIONSHIP LETTER TO YOUR PARENTS

If you have a rocky relationship with your folks—and you'd like to make it better—then consider writing them a letter. In your own words, try to comment on each of the following points.

1. Express your gratitude for all that your folks do—and have done—for you. Be sure to mention how they provide for you (money, clothes, food, travel), how they offer you wise counsel, how they show their love for you, and how they demonstrate patience when you mess up.

2. If there's some ongoing fight or unresolved issue between you and your parents, then own up to your part in it. Use words of confession, clearly saying something like, "I did this, and it was wrong." Then use words of contrition, emphasizing that you're sorry for the pain and stress you caused them. Finally, use words of reconciliation,

making the point that you'd like to have a closer, better relationship with your folks in the future.

3. If you've been angry or resentful over something your parents did to you—either years ago or more recently—then find a way to tell them you've been carrying some resentment toward them and you'd like to forgive them and let go of the emotional baggage. Make it clear that you're not necessarily asking them to apologize to you, just that you want to get past the situation in your own life.

Note: Don't include section three unless you really mean it. As Jesus-followers the big idea is to understand how much God has forgiven us—and that, by comparison, no one has done as much to us as we've done to God with our sin. Not forgiving others is making light of God's forgiveness of us. However, forgiveness can be a very

difficult issue—especially if major hurt is involved. Don't include this paragraph if you're not ready to go there. Instead, spend some time in Ephesians 4:32 and Matthew 18:21-35.

4. Ask your parents what you can do to make your relationship with them stronger. Be honest in saying that you're willing to listen to any suggestions or comments they have to offer.

Before you give your parents the letter, make sure you understand that it's a very humbling document. Spend some time in prayer and make sure your heart is in the same place as the words of your letter. Ask God to help you to be grateful for your parents, to be honest with them, and to be responsive to their wisdom.

CHAPTER 12
CASE STUDIES

Here are some real-life scenarios involving teenagers and their parents, followed by a list of possible responses. What would you do in each situation? What would you *want* to do? What would you do if you were living as a Jesus-follower?

THE CAMPOUT

A group of guys and girls are driving out to the lake to camp out together overnight. Toby really wants to go, but he knows his mom will say no if he tells her there are girls going.

OPTIONS

a. Toby doesn't even bother asking because he already knows the answer.

b. Toby tells his mom the whole story and makes his case for why he's mature enough to handle a co-ed overnight campout.

c. Toby tells his mom about the outing,

but he doesn't mention that there will be girls there.

d. Toby says nothing and sneaks out of the house after his mom has gone to bed.

e. Toby lies about his age, joins the Marines, and gets a tattoo.

WARDROBE ISSUES

Linda's dad is really sensitive about how Linda dresses. He's always making her change her skirt or top. It's embarrassing to Linda—especially when he tells her right in front of her friends to change her clothes before she leaves the house.

OPTIONS

a. Linda screams at her dad every time he asks her to change her clothes, and she slams the door of her room for emphasis.

b. Linda talks to her dad, acknowledges that he has the authority to ask her to change, but asks that he not do it in front of her friends.

c. Linda asks her dad for a more specific standard of what's okay so she can stop wasting his money on clothes that he won't let her wear out of the house.

d. Linda protests by wearing a bulky, ankle-length, high-necked dress for a week.

BAD INFLUENCE

Marie has been spending a lot of time with her friend Tanya, even though she knows her mom thinks Tanya is a bad influence. Marie can see why her mom thinks that, but she also believes she has an opportunity to be a good influence on Tanya. In a heated argument, her mom finally says, "You can't hang out with Tanya anymore."

OPTIONS

a. Marie screams at her mom and doesn't talk to her for a week, but she also obeys and stays away from Tanya.

b. Marie says, "Okay, Mom, you're the boss. I appreciate your concern." Then she continues to hang out with Tanya and lies about it to her mom.

c. Marie doesn't like her mom's decision and makes that clear to her mom, but she also accepts it because there's nothing else she can do.

d. Marie comes up with a creative alternative and asks her mom: "What if I only hang out with Tanya at our house or at youth group functions?"

MAD DAD

Thad has a problem. His dad is angry and aloof all the time. Thad's mom and dad have been fighting a lot. And anytime Thad asks his dad for anything, his dad just says "No" or blows his stack.

OPTIONS

a. Thad thinks, *Fine. I'll just stay away from him from now on. It's his problem, not mine.*

b. Thad prays for his dad and asks God to make his dad less of a selfish jerk so the family won't be so stressed out.

c. Thad prays for his dad and asks God to help Thad's dad relax, recognize that God loves him, and treat Thad's mom better.

d. Thad asks his pastor and all the church elders to organize a surprise intervention for his dad at work.

CHAPTER 13

FINAL NOTE: WHEN PARENTS ARE ABUSIVE

I

f you're in an abusive relationship with your parents, I want to say as clearly as I can that what's happening (or has happened) to you is not okay. I've written this book for students who have a pretty good, if sometimes difficult, relationship with their folks. If you've been reading along and wondering how any of this could ever work in your home, then you might have a good reason to wonder. Let me tell you what I say to kids who reveal to me that their parents are being abusive.

First, it's wrong. No parent should abuse a child (of any age) physically, sexually, or even verbally through intentionally hurtful insults, swearing, and mean mocking. It's *always* wrong *all the time*. The God who tells you to honor and obey your parents doesn't mean for you to submit to abuse. It's not okay for them to do those things to you. And it's not okay for them to do it to a spouse, either.

Second, it's not your fault. Many abused kids have a hard time believing that. No parent hits or molests or abuses their kids because the kids are bad. The problem always lies with the abuser. No matter what you've done or haven't done, you don't deserve to be abused.

Third, God loves you deeply. The way you've been hurt makes him both sad and very angry. Jesus said, "If anyone causes one of these little ones who believe in me to sin, it would be better for him to have a large millstone hung around his neck and to be drowned in the depths of the sea" (Matthew 18:6). If Jesus felt that way about an adult leading a child into sin, imagine how he feels about an adult abusing a child. The book of Proverbs makes it very clear that God hates it when the innocent are hurt by the powerful. That's what

has happened to you, and God doesn't take it lightly.

Fourth, it's not wrong for you to get help. It's not disobedient to tell someone about this. You won't be dishonoring your hurtful parent. In fact, your parent needs to be stopped for his own good. If there's any hope for him, he'll one day regret and weep over what he's done. But in order to get to that point, he needs to be caught, stopped, given a chance (away from you, for now) to get help, and pay for his crime. Your choice to tell someone is an act of love for your parent.

Fifth, you *must* tell someone. Please contact a counselor or a youth pastor or a pastor or a teacher. All of those people are required by law to report to the authorities what you tell them. A good pastor or youth leader could also get you some help to begin the long process of healing from your abuse.

Finally, God's love for you is real. God wanted to have you home with him so badly that he was willing to sacrifice his own Son to give you that chance. I realize some abused people don't like to hear that God is their Father because they can only picture dads as hurtful people. But a friend of mine with a painful background once told me that he didn't see it that way. He said it was obvious to him from observing his friends' dads that his own dad wasn't "good." He longed for a good dad. There is no better dad than your Father in heaven.

Please contact an adult you can trust and start the process of ending the pain. It *can* end, and you're strong enough to do something about it. Everyone reading the words in this book wants you to do that, and many of them are praying that you will.

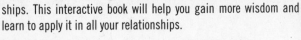

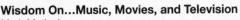